Of Smoke Flesh and Bone:

Poetry Against Depression

Abigail George

Edited by Antonio Garcia

Mwanaka Media and Publishing Pvt Ltd,
Chitungwiza Zimbabwe

*

Creativity, Wisdom and Beauty

Publisher: Mmap
Mwanaka Media and Publishing Pvt Ltd
24 Svosve Road, Zengeza 1
Chitungwiza Zimbabwe
mwanaka@yahoo.com
www.africanbookscollective.com/publishers/mwanaka-media-and-publishing
https://facebook.com/MwanakaMediaAndPublishing/

Distributed in and outside N. America by African Books Collective
orders@africanbookscollective.com
www.africanbookscollective.com

ISBN: 978-1-77929-597-2
EAN: 9781779295972

©Abigail George 2020

All rights reserved.
No part of this book may be reproduced or transmitted in any form or by any means, mechanical or electronic, including photocopying and recording, or be stored in any information storage or retrieval system, without written permission from the publisher

DISCLAIMER
All views expressed in this publication are those of the author and do not necessarily reflect the views of Mmap.

Mwanaka Media and Publishing Editorial Board:

Publisher/ Editor-in-Chief: Tendai Rinos Mwanaka
mwanaka13@gmail.com
East Africa and Swahili Literature: Dr Wanjohiwa Makokha
makokha.justus@ku.ac.ke
East Africa English Literature: Andrew Nyongesa (PhD student)
nyongesa55.andrew@gmail.com
East Africa and Children Literature: Richard Mbuthia
ritchmbuthia@gmail.com
Legal Studies and Zimbabwean Literature: Jabulani Mzinyathi
jabumzi@gmail.com
Economics, Development, Environment and Zimbabwean Literature: Dr UshehweduKufakurinaniushehwedu@gmail.com
History, Politics, International relations and South African Literature: Antonio Garcia antoniogarcia81@yahoo.com
North African and Arabic Literature:FethiSassisassifathi62@yahoo.fr
Gender and South African Literature: Abigail George
abigailgeorge79@gmail.com
Francophone and South West African Literature: Nsah Mala
nsahmala@gmail.com
West Africa Literature: Macpherson Okparachiefmacphersoncritic@gmail.com
Media studies and South African Literature: Mikateko Mbambo
me.mbambo@gmail.com
Portuguese and West Africa Literature: Daniel da Purificação
danieljose26@yahoo.com.br

Also by this author

Africa Where Art Thou
Feeding the Beasts
All about My Mother
Winter in Johannesburg
Brother Wolf and Sister Wren
Sleeping Under the Kitchen Tables in the Northern Areas
The Scholarship Girl
Parks and Recreation

Dedication

For Richard Ali, Christina Deptula, Dimitris Giannakopoulos, Sam Hawksmoor, Thanos Kalamidas, Nyambura Kiarie, Justin Lowe, Naza Amaeze Okoli and Solo Osofisan, with love and much respect.

Acknowledgements

I'd just like to take this opportunity to thank some important people in my life. Friends, loves, family, who gave up their time for me. Thank you for your vision, wisdom and for being you. For Amatoritsero Ede, Mbizo Chirasha, Chika Onyenezi, Chimee Adioha, Chimamanda Ngozi Adichie, even though we have never met, I consider her to be one of the greatest writers of her generation. This book is also for the Dutch poet Joop Bersee (a rare and giving talent), the editor, translator, mentor and poet Douglas Reid Skinner, cherished friend, gifted man and epic filmmaker David Max Brown of Noem My Skollie (Call Me Thief) fame, the brilliant editor, ringleader of the African Renaissance in Zimbabwe and on this side of the world and publisher of my book *The Scholarship Girl* Tendai Rinos Mwanaka, Antonio "Tony" Garcia my editor- I have nothing but praise for you (thank you for your patience), for Toast Coetzer who gave me a chance to try my hand at travel writing (I will be eternally grateful to you for believing in me). I am also indebted and grateful to Sand Pilarski who published many of my poems in Piker Press and Brian Walter who played mentor in my life and who is also a multi-award-winning poet.

    I am also grateful to Dr Shaheed Hendricks, Dr Aminah Hendricks and Dr Farah Hendricks. The Hendricks family has been such a blessing to me and my father Dr Ambrose Cato George over this past year. I thank Pat King, prayer warrior, faithful servant and powerful man of God. For my mother Gerda who taught me that hope has a mystical agenda all of its own. That it has its own shelf-life, its own rules. Thank you mummy for teaching me that miracles do occur when you least expect it and that miracles can be achieved when you believe in the impossible. For Ursula Candasamy, Babs, Diana Ferrus, Shelley Barry, Laura M. Kaminski, yes, I am thanking you all for inspiring me. You're all fiercely independent, helluva women and beautiful souls, inside-and-out. Thank you for being in my life. To the divine, to heaven and hell, to creativity and creative-assignments, to imagination, friendship and to love, to my room with a view, my actor-loves, my poet-loves, my writing-loves, my filmmaker-loves, talk-show host-loves, my political loves, Kwame Nkrumah, Patrice Lumumba, Julius Malema, Stephen Bantu Biko, Sexton and Plath, Ted Hughes, Robert Lowell, Rupert Brooke, F. Scott Fitzgerald, Ernest Hemingway, Marianne Williamson, Oprah Winfrey, Thandie Newton, Onyeka Nwelue, Sisonke Msimang, James Franco, John Updike, Jerome David Salinger, Anele Mdoda, Trevor Noah, Rainer Maria Rilke, T.S. Eliot, Ezra Pound, Vladimir Nabokov, Vincent van Gogh, M. Night Shyamalan, Stanley Kubrick, Diane Arbus, Nicole Kidman, Sofia Coppola, Kathryn Bigelow, Adeline Virginia Woolf, Rebecca Miller's "personal velocity" as screenwriter, Daniel Day Lewis, Andre Brink, Richard Rive and Ingrid Jonker. For Allan Kolski Horwitz, Robert Berold, Gavin Hood, Terry Pheto, Vonani Bila, Ayanda Billie, Mxolisi Nyezwa, Mzi Mahola, Monde Ngoyama, Zhimkulu Fatman, Deon Bender, Oom Frans, Akin Omotosa, Arja Salafranca, Cornelia Fick who all showed me the way forward and for all my beloved speech and drama teachers, the late Marjorie Gilbey, Sharon Rother and Linda Louise Swain.

This also goes out to the love of my life Shakespeare, my beacon John Keats, my anchor Bessie Head, my inspiration for the perfect working relationship of Gertrude Stein and Alice B. Toklas. For those who are drawn to writing about the broken-hearted, for those that live to write, that believe that writing is always another country, that writing is the unknown, a pause between two acts, an interlude. To all who drink coffee first thing in the morning to start the creative process and juices flowing, to all who journal, to all who have a hunger for the African Renaissance, to all who have a hunger for Hemingway's Paris and bookstores and libraries and well-loved, well-thumbed first editions and charity shops that belong to the bone marrow of the poet-writer. A special thanks goes out to all the healthcare professionals at Helen Joseph, Elizabeth Donkin, Garden City Clinic, Hunterscraig, Tara, and Valkenburg.

Table of Contents

Also by this author..iv
Dedication..v
Acknowledgements..vi
Foreword..xi
Editor's Preface..xiv
Struggles...1
Ingrid Jonker's Black Butterflies...........................2
Depression..6
Please don't think about this, love........................8
Yes, you heal the ground I walk on.....................10
Wherever the soul comes from...........................12
If you want to write, write, don't be a ghost......13
The theft of George Botha's silence....................15
Your grandfather and winter trees in London...17
As I came home...18
The city lights of Port Elizabeth or take my hand if you're afraid...21
Miracles..23
Anne Sexton Renaissance woman.......................24
Stranger made of flesh and Nineveh...................28
The packed suitcase...30
The bone slums...32
Because a ghost was in my blood........................34
A month of Sundays and prayers........................36
Must travel...38
Gone to Jean Rhys' purple sea.............................39
For everything my parents taught me................40
The argument...42
The infant...44
Ascension...45
Rain..47
Teaching...49

Virginia Woolf in the Flesh..50
Quiver..54
Daughters and their fathers..56
A woman at work..58
The red-sparrow instinct of the phoenix.............................60
As I stand in this empty space..62
To the resting place of the lighthouse.................................64
When the philosopher came into my life............................66
Just looking for a place to rest my head.............................68
Things you need to know about stardust............................70
Karma..72
Assia Wevill...73
A drought of words in a journal..77
Behold the glory of the river 78
Winter leaf and the smell of apples...................................80
Tenderness and extraordinary vertigo...............................82
Shelter and protection..84
Hive...87
The painted birds...89
All about Eve...91
All my life Rilke in my hands...93
In expectation of you showing up.....................................95
The nature of things...97
The Split Personalities of Elizabeth Donkin......................98
Mmap New African Poets Series....................................104

Foreword

"My grief is published here on the page," says Abigail George in one of her poems ['Because a ghost was in my blood'] and I believe her. The raw honesty of her feelings – not just grief but also anger, frustration, longing, hope, confusion, aging, love, depression – is evident throughout this new collection, a fact that might cause the reader to feel both awkwardly uncomfortable and, perhaps paradoxically, deeply reassured.

Her several identities as woman, daughter, sister, writer are clearly a single identity although this is expressed variously at different times, in different ways, and in different poems. In fact, this remarkable short collection seems almost like the writer's struggle to find out which of her disparate personas is the 'real' one, and yet the strange thing is that the very richness of this complexity creates her uniqueness. And these poems are unique.

Personifying 'Depression' as a lover who "runs me a/ Bath after a long day" and who "Knows how I like my coffee first thing/In the morning", yet whose "eyes are flint. Heart made out of/The air of a clock", she brings substance to a truly painful condition from which so many people suffer without having the means to deal with it. Maybe poetry of this honesty and distinction can help. The importance of family relationships reverberates through the poems – an urgent need for a familial perfection that often doesn't reveal itself. And the agony of fervently wishing, longing for an acceptance never quite achieved is everywhere:

> I'm standing at the door of the church
> hall. Waiting.
>   Pretending that I've been invited to the party.
> That I fit in. That I can sing.

['The packed suitcase']

So, yes: loneliness. That's the word that rises steadily from these pages; but it's a loneliness firmly combined with the resolute courage to face and move past it, to write it into submission.

These poems are brave. Interestingly, much of their power is reinforced by their physical appearance on the page, their shape, the 'itch' of their formatting. Line breaks often seem to stretch all the rules, lines ending on 'weak' words – conjunctions, articles, pronouns – as if to emphasise the awkwardness, the discomfort, of the emotions involved. And it works. I began reading each poem with a slightly suspicious curiosity about this technique but ended in warm appreciation and enjoyment. They are good.

A number also refer, either directly or indirectly, to other introspective writers – Virginia Woolf and Jean Rhys, for instance, as well as the Dutch poet Joop Bersee–the implication being that the process of writing can offer psychological support in coming to terms with life's vicissitudes. I wouldn't argue.

So when, in 'Stranger made of flesh and Nineveh', the poet writes "I'm crying, and I don't know why I'm crying", she is writing for more than the 'I' speaking in the poem – she speaks for all of us who have experienced such enervating emotional paralysis. This is the power of her poetry: it reaches out beyond itself with an empathetic generosity that our world so badly needs. And it ends, appropriately, in courage and hope:

> I have reading
> Hands. Her storm river mouth is not
> Quite as alien to me as it once was. She's a leap of faith
> That I need to take into the wild.

['A month of Sundays and prayers']

Harry Owen
18/10/2018

Poet Laureate, for Cheshire in 2003

Editor's Preface

In this striking work, Abigail puts forward a brave and powerful collection of poems. This book contains Abigail's letter to the world – an account of her pain, love, passion and inspiration. Poets interpret the world through their lens. They make sense of their experiences using creative expression and give a voice to the often unexplored, raw and complex parts of human existence.

Abigail allows the reader into her world and shares her battle with depression. In an intimate display of artistic ability, she lets us into her world and shares her suffering, her battle and her joy. Abigail is unafraid of revealing herself to society, she challenges the reader to look into her life. How could we understand another's circumstance? Do we dare to reach into an unknown world? This book is an invitation into the soul of a modern poet.

Abigail announces herself with each poem. Always personal, raw and proud. She is not confined by cadence, rhyme and rhythm. She breaks rules and makes new ones, she writes from the heart, which becomes the metronome of each line. The words hurt, grate and soothe at once creating distance and bringing the reader closer to a world far away.

In a moment where society, or at least some part of it, wants to be more inclusive, this work is a window into depression. Her beautiful poetry shows us how creation and art is not limited to a certain portion of society and how we all can relate to common themes.

Abigail has structured her work into four main sections 'struggles', 'miracles', 'teaching', karma and 'the nature of things'. Each section is introduced through a short story and shows us a different part of Abigail. The division of the poetry is not mutually exclusive, and are not categorised into well-defined packets, but are rather shaped by overlapping themes. They represent the mind, and the heart which unapologetically thinks and feels at the same time.

Antonio Garcia

February 2019

Struggles

In this section I show you my inner world. I reveal my battle with depression. It is the opposite of logical. I reach, I fall short, I overshoot, and I continue. It never ends, a balancing act of competing feelings and moments.

Ingrid Jonker's Black Butterflies

Let us tell ghost stories.

Jonker is a ghost of her former self, but she is still in the land of the living — a tragic beauty in a state of personal turmoil and crisis.

"There is no time like the future to seal my fate," she thinks to herself, with growing uncertainty. She is unbearably nervous tonight. She fidgets. Her fingers twitch. The clock on the wall opposite her distracts her and she smokes cigarette after cigarette and then dashes them in an ashtray. She feels exposed, she paces up and down, but she still attaches no serious damage or blame to her last love affair. She was gentle and loving with her small daughter, Simone today. Simone is a beautiful child. Sweet and well behaved.

In Paris, she was already a writer in exile — cursed, perturbed and a voyeur who had high-maintenance tastes. She is still unclear about what she is going to do about her lover. Her resolve unravelled that night in the flat. Her beauty meant nothing to her. She was not conceited. What had her attractive looks brought her but ill-fated relationships, rejection, pain and suffering? Nothing dulled or sated her desire for love, for life, for a hot and heavy intellectual debate, which her voice was the centre of. In retrospect, living in Apartheid, participating in conversations with other coloured and black writers, poets and intellectuals at secret literary meetings had made her begin to doubt what she was living for.

She wanted to be taken seriously as a woman, but more importantly, as a writer. They were dangerously in hate with a patriarchal system. The essence of the identity being passed to her was a fate worse than death and could not guarantee security in her chosen field or career.

Love will change you in an indescribable way. It will make the strong weak, strong hearts weak, render the intellectual speechless, comedians will vanish and be replaced by philosophers; the funny will be replaced by philosophy and everything that was laughable before is serious and stimulating. The challenges of the human condition become painfully obvious. Death is the ultimate sacrifice, invisible and mysterious. Ingrid Jonker made a decision for herself that was useless.

There is no earthly justification for what she did. Removing the very substance of her gift, her genius from this world, by taking her own life, by drowning herself in the sea.

As they pulled the limp body from the ocean, the subject in death mirrored life. There was a chill in her embrace. Her fingers were numb. She was haunting, pale and beautiful, lacking tenderness. Her cheeks were wet as if from tears. Her mouth is full. Her lips are cool, as if she has drunk her fill. Her appetite is sated. She sleeps to dream, she does not speak and there is no lapsed recovery from the multiple meanings of words. There will no longer be the willing prerogative of an insomniac to stay up the whole night and blot out the stain of her sins by writing.

The male police officers' hair was windswept. They talked amongst themselves.

The breeze was salty, the morning tide came in, the breakers crashed against the rocks, the foam raced towards the shore, birds circling overhead perched on rocks and altered states were trapped in a war of nerves. Her eyes stared into the pale, blue sky. The beginning of the day was like her work, imaginative. It gave recognition to curious incidents in the still, mournful air of the morning. It concerned itself with the decline of evil and the harmful beginnings of the harvest of desolation.

The shadow of a ghost of a haunting memory refused to disappear into a hazy reverie. The poet, Ingrid Jonker, is dead. Her face has an unsmiling seriousness on it. Even in death, she is angelic. Her demeanour never giving way to the trouble or unfounded insecurity that lay underneath.

She is authentic, a true original, a unique. She will never know this in her own lifetime. Her life when held up to scrutiny in death will revere it. She knew what the imagination was capable of, the loneliness of the heart and when it was ready to surrender to a temporary escape into a romance. Her innocence and vulnerability remind me of women ahead of the times they were born into, women who were visionaries, leaders, and had to endure great humiliation from powerful men, women from a more traditional public realm. Women like Joan of Arc, Saartjie Baartman, Susan Sontag, Princess Diana, Sylvia Plath and Marilyn Monroe.

She is barefoot in her flat. Her hair is dark, wild and free and falls across her face. Yet in her eyes, there is a declaration of having been to hell and back again. There has been a radical change in her behaviour since she came back from Paris that has not escaped her but she does not speak of her experiences there, of the lingering sadness that torments her. The 'unhappiness' does not have a name yet, but soon the world will know and there is nothing she can do to protect her daughter from it.

Fate is like a drowned thing, an empty shell reserved for the sound of silence invoking the sound of the ocean. She has decided she is a poor activist, wife, mother, woman and lover. Simone, her daughter, wants to make her smile but she is tired of playing games.

Nonetheless she plays along, pretends to catch the joke, and today, when the journalist came for the interview, there was a glimmer of a smile on her face when her picture was taken. The picture of her as the famous, prize-winning poet. 'The female voice of her generation' was a small consolation to her. Without her father's love, she felt lost. Fame meant little or nothing to her and the turning point came now, this night. How different would things be in the morning for people that she had been estranged from for years, she wondered quietly to herself?

How many times, I wonder, did she have to redirect her focus when tears blurred her vision when she cried, when she was working? How do you survive a blessed and cursed childhood? What made her laugh, this sensitive, delicate woman? Who made her smile? The elementary particles of light became diffused on her face. It was translucent, her face was dreamy and her lashes were damp. There is a distracting air near the incident now as they wait for the coroner. Simone woke up in the stillness of the flat and went in search of her mother. She searched the rooms one by one and found that they were empty.

Where does this story begin? The car is hurtling down the road past everything a young Ingrid knows and loves. This is the world of a child, a babyish language, tea parties in the shade with her sister, barefoot on the sandy beach searching for beautiful feathers, smooth pebbles and colourful shells. Now history has turned the page. Their father has come to fetch them to live with him and his family. Their idyllic childhood is over forever.

Depression

My depression has its own voice.
He wears a crown of winter leaves.
He is my companion, my lover,
My after-thought. It is always winter
When he is near. In bed his arms
Always reach for me. He runs me a
Bath after a long day. Sometimes I
Put on make-up for him to cover up
The blue feeling that holds me down
From the top of my head to the
Soles of my feet. He tells me in no uncertain
Terms that I should wear perfume
More often. I should play tennis like I
Used to. I should go swimming. I should
Take long walks. I should fall in love.
I should have a relationship to take my
Mind away from him but I laugh at this.
He knows by now I don't take him

Seriously at all. Doctors say he is a
Hazard to my health. I should pay
Attention to what they tell me. It's
For my own good. But I've lived with
Him for years now. I'm used to his
Ways and he is used to mine. He knows
The time I get up (usually late morning).
He knows my writing routine. He
Knows how I like my coffee first thing
In the morning. My tea as the hours
Pass into evening. We draw up plans
And lists together. It's a joy to map out

A fixed day. We laugh together.
We cry together. We share everything.
He is a glacier. Tension underneath the surface.
He is sunburn, feather, and gull in the air.
His eyes are flint. Heart made out of
The air of a clock. I know him so well.

Please don't think about this, love

You're bone-thin. Come drink a glass of
wine with me to fatten up your bones. The
monsters sitting around this kitchen table
are sinful creatures. They remember their
table manners but nothing else. Many things
were left unsaid by my mother after I left
home. She did not say that she would miss
me. That she would always love me. The
leaves are singing holy. The spring in my
step is holy. I'm stepping over stones. Monsters
at my back. Blood in my veins, a seawall
that makes up my chest, (blood) rays of
light in my eyes, and teachings in my hands.
My strange feet accused of not always taking
me where I want to go. Now, sister, you're
like a splinter in driftwood in my finger.
I have to get you out. Out! Even ripened
thunder is a teacher. The virgins are like
angels here. I have to let go of your grip,
but I can't. You perfect me. Instruct me. I
pray fiercely that there'll be enough room
for you in this world one day. That this hurt
in my wrists will go away. Glory is small
when humane winners take it all. You're

in everything that I see, sister. You're the vine,
I'm the branch. You're your own love story.
Here the light of day scares me because there's

so little of it. Just a few grains scattered here

and there. Waking up alone doesn't scare me
anymore though. I've done it now for most of

my life. Rilke, Updike are my warriors of support
now, and I tremble at the thought of how chameleon-
like we are. Water, the material, earth, they all

have their own essence. And their own psychology,
and education. Even lovers understand this.
The moonlight shifting like the tides. Rivers.

I have dahlias in my hands. Accept them, then
you will accept me. I don't think it much to ask.

Yes, you heal the ground I walk on

You heal the ground I walk on. All the quiet

things that my heart desires. This is a face
that tells the truth. I tell myself whenever I
look to you. There are tiny beads of light in
your eyes. You taught me that we express
ourselves in writing about our thoughts. It's
extraordinary to think just how far we've come
in such a short space of time. You're lovely.
Kind. Your knowledge is sublime. Abundance
in nature where I live is festive this time of
year. You're the most vulnerable. Strong
stems from strong. Stories stem from pain's
metaphors, dirt and grace, the worship of the
earth, and the praise of nightfall. I want to
tell you that I've known pain, but I can't. That
sometimes there's an animal inside of me.
Up close it keeps its confidence, and a long
silence. I want to stop this weeping, but I can't.

You're farthest from my mind now, sister.
The root of fear, call it a shroud. The cloak
and dagger game. Let this monkish branch
unearth this truth about life, the angels, and
the humanity that comes with maturity, and
confidence. Gone are the days of mother, and
father acting passionately towards each other.
Now they sleep in separate beds. And so, I
watch you blossom, and slowly fade away. I

find Neville Alexander, Dulcie September,

Jakes Gerwel in this angelic vineyard. Dusk. Moonlight on your face, a prize. I find you all there.

Wherever the soul comes from

I have to stop living in this torment if only
for you. I have to begin to live in gratitude
more. This eternity that I think lifts only
when I write. Can you translate this for me,
or tell me what it is about. I only write in
English, and understand English, but I don't
mean to sound arrogant. Sorry if I sound
arrogant. I don't mean to be selfish. Sorry
if I sound selfish. There are people in this
world who play holy. Sorry if I come across
like that. All I know is that all poets are
anointed, holy, and sacred no matter what
language they write in, and like you I am
also grand by the way. You wrote a very
fine poem. Thank you for your honesty, and
please stay in touch, sir. Send me another poem.
I'm writing a series of poems on sobriety.

Sister says this house is a palace. Brother
was calm today, and I, I wait. I wait for
the white fields of snow that come in winter.
I lock the backdoor at night. Check all the
doors. I drink sister's tea. Brother made a
cross when he came out of rehab. He fashioned
it out of fallen branches. A rusty nail holds
it together. And very soon all our lives became
like that cross. Brother became determined
to live, and not give up. He was the eye of the tiger,
and we all lived to become theologians.

We became like chameleons, and all of our winters

soon turned into summers in his hands.

If you want to write, write, don't be a ghost

You can see it if you look closely enough. Even the comets step out in faith. The meteors. People. Volcanoes. Even the patterns on your flesh have a complex. Prayer to me is like air. My reading hands are greedy for the sunlight. The palace of the sun. The sun, well, she's moving. Revelatory. Even the holy is visible here. I can see it. I can see it. I'm full of laughter and tears. My heart is open. Willing to share the inheritance of futility and loss found there in the silence and the empty rooms of my childhood house. I think of how I know the tastes of childhood trauma, like I know the smell of spaghetti. It's an ancient landscape. Seldom glorious unless it is overcome. I think of the therapists I've been to, how many of them have been Indian women, and beautiful. I think of class and speaking English proper all my life. I think of my sadness, and then I think of you. Now let me talk about broken families. Your wit is warm-hearted but your heart is condescending and cold. You call me up when you're lonely. You're digging, digging, digging into me, and I'm branching out into particles. We have to tell our stories. The leaves here are holy. Sister has a voice of longing. Brother's clothes are on the bedroom floor. I

live in mother's house. She wants me gone like
yesterday. I think that the gifts of humanity are

like the ocean. That same ocean also belongs to
my mother. The sadness that was there before is
gone now. I am caught up in a dream. I have yet

to find a being to be with, live a lifetime with,
settle down, marry, and have those children with
the angelic shine on their faces. Thank you for

not calling. Thank you for not texting me. Thank
you for this long silence. For this pain. I think of
the fact that I am no longer afraid to close my eyes.

You were something beautiful. An altar. I think of
the retreat of solitude and futility. Their exposure.
Lava. The anointed. Wherever the soul comes from.

The theft of George Botha's silence

Comrade, elsewhere
there's progress in a distillate
that can't be erased
from public life. "Man for all seasons".
After silence I'm
caught between the wires of
the rise and decline of apartheid.
The decline and fall
of an empire. Tidal.
Its aftermath windswept
with integral bridges.
Out there cities plural,

it's a landscape of graves.
The brilliant gone long
before their time. Comrades,
countrymen, countrywomen.
They're welcomed
into eternity even
though they're more
ghost than ash, dirt, clay, earth, soil.
Afterwards, I feel
a kind of emptiness inside.
As if I've been hollowed
out with fingers.

He's an atom. He's an angel
whose sins have been
washed away. His
hands are clean as
snow. He's wind

and sky and rain
without a soul. The
forecast says that
he's a weathered particle with velocity.
Listen, he's a symphony.
A Masai warrior's feet
in the dust. He's independent
of the river. I can taste
his truth. Its light. Salt.

Your grandfather and winter trees in London

My dearest boy. My sweet child. There's a
Long road to spirituality. A quartet, a feast.

A moveable feast, an ex-President Thabo Mbeki, John Nash,
Jerome David Salinger. You're fed stories
About ghosts and zombie princesses by me.
Nothing but rusk and rooibos tea with milk.
Angel face I don't want you to end up a broken
Man. I want you to hold a map in your hands
For all your life. Black is the water. Black is
Winter. The suffering. Poverty. I think of the
Depths of the ocean with fifty different kinds
Of vision. You're the sea. You're the sea. To me
Though you're dry grass. You're dry grass.
It's lovely to dream. To know that you're mine.
Part of me. Even my anguish and loneliness.
Even my powers of what I find relevant, and yes,
Even my pain. I am all-powerful. As powerful
As any single and intelligent woman nearing
Her forties can be. It's a gift. It's a gift. Born
Knowing. Acknowledging freedom. The heat
Of regret can damage. You looked at me through
Another man's eyes and said what a waste of
A human life if you do not live, laugh, love,
Socialize, but I could not, will not yield to that.
It will destroy me if I did any of that but you
Don't understand. I do know joy but only in writing
About life and the last person I have ever truly

Loved. I think of Grahamstown, Swaziland,
Montagu and Sedgefield and what the future holds

For me. Weeping passes through me. Sobs. It's
Not as if I show regret on my face the morning
After anymore. I still know your name. That you're
Great at what you do. All I want to do is catch
Up to the winter sun. All I want is to know you again.
But you're not my man. You're not my boy. You're
Not mine but now I must speak in a language
Every mother understands. You're Truman Capote's
Music. You're climate and mockingbird. You're
Humming my kind of blues. Yes, I'll remember
You in the same way I've loved every man who has
Entered my life. Take a bow. I think of the light
That swimmers' must have in their eyes at the local
Swimming pool and I begin to write poetry.
Words come. They come and I write. Words come and
I write. I think of when I started to write this
Book. It would be so wrong to write only about
Love, or only about despair, and then I think
Back to what inspired me in the first place.
The tiny well that we dug up in the grass at the
Back of the house where I buried the limp body
Of your kitten and how it was mostly your grandfather
Who wanted to keep it a secret from you.

As I came home

Even when it hurts like the sun. The spark
of manhood or woman-speak. Even when
it hurts gulls made of flame on an island.
Even when it hurts glaring or silence and

tears. Even when it hurts treacherous smoke
or clouds. Even when it hurts arrows or a
shore-less continent. Even when it hurts love
or swept away sea or wound. The tall,

green-shifting universe is all proof I need
that once I was loved by you. My hands are
lonely. Beneath me lies gracious fury. At
the end of the day, I find a mountain there.

Robert Louis Stevenson wrote poems. Rudyard
Kipling. Thomas Hardy. At the end of suffering
comes joy. At the beach, I watch seawalls
fall. Man, beast, bird bodiless from where

I stand except the English poet Rupert Brooke.
Except Rome. Finding the source of the Nile.
I turn my eyes to see your liquid eyes. Your
sun-like face and I wonder who your God is.

I'm tired with work and suffering. Rain
waters the scorched earth. Lust can comfort
us in primitive and savage ways. I think
of the bottom of the world. More beautiful than words can
ever say. I think of the crying of a wild
bird. The loneliness found in a city. The

shining centre of the earth brighter than
the sun. The devil is a ruthless creature that
mocks the non-humanity in all of us. It is
Christ that possesses me entirely, completely.
I think of those inheriting control. Those

fetching angels that have taught me that
guilt is a lifeless unruly whirlwind. All I
see is thin people wearing enigmatic smiles
eating air on the covers of magazines
with self-mastery. Icy people with lofty
ambitions but I am not one of them. He
looks older, more handsome with the beard.
I could start my life over with somebody
new but my brain tells me we'll probably
be strangers for the rest of our lives.
Reading has taught me that even solitude
can be miraculous. Futility. Loneliness.

The city lights of Port Elizabeth or take my hand if you're afraid

All the bare necessities of writing

are found at an empty table. Figs and tea.
The flame of language is found there. Hot
ink. Writing. Prayer. People are found
milling in gardens in the summer heat drinking.
Eating good cheese and bread because
it is the season of eating good cheese
and bread. The writer hovers. He belongs.
She belongs but she is not part of the
group. She's just an observer. Writers
watch through the window. Watching
the voices until there's nothing but the heat.
Burning Midwest prairies. Cacti in desert-land.
Thirsty for thin black veils to cover the ocean-wind and sea
that aren't found there. Only sky. Only
sky. Creeping up like sunlight. Everything
happened so fast. Oh, insane rapture's
shadowboxing game! This honey in the
blood. This evil-sound of weeping. This smoke
kissing springtime courage and harsh
anguish silent all these years. Now there's

all this expectation. Rewrites of heart-

ache on my body. Seduction theories.
I had solitude. I wanted disasters to be
kind to me. I was alive even in those
empty moments. I brought submission to the kitchen table.

The neon light is lovely here. The city
lights of Port Elizabeth a blessing. A man's
heart is gold. A woman's heart sacred
machine. Sad girl listen for the birdsong

in Tokyo. All I want is a library to keep
me warm on my voyage to China away
from this country of tragedy. The wedding
of leaf and darkness is closing in. You'll

find monsters at the deep end. They're
there at the edge of the city lights if you
look hard enough. You'll find the auras
of soil and water. Dust and heat. The photograph of an artist in her
hands.

Remember the tranquil daylight. Then finally
death. Don't be frightened to close your eyes to it.

Miracles

This world is shaped by tragedy. It is love and the constant search for a better tomorrow which gives us hope. I challenge myself to find a miracle in all things.

Anne Sexton Renaissance-woman

When you are a manic-depressive, you are married to your fears, your anxieties, your insecurities.

Up and down your moods will go. Of course, in the end you will become addicted to something. Alcohol, over the counter medication, barbiturates, and food anything just to bring closure. Even my throat has a pattern. A pattern of the blue cut glass of the sky. It is not just emptiness filled with vowels and consonants. It smells of perfume. I want comfort but I also want anger. I want the progeny. I want to be the scholar of trivia. I want the white picket fence. I want that station wagon. I want those daughters who will be my heirs. I want that husband but I realise this. I am aware of that I cannot have those visions and be the drowning visitor in winter every year.

Love me or hate me. Like me or dislike me. I do not really care. For me to exist, I sometimes must sigh very loudly or exhale very deeply drawing attention to myself. I know other women will think that I must have everything that my heart desires but then again who is the real phony there. I am beautiful. There I said it. No turning back now. I married. I had those kids. I had that sunny road and then the heavens opened up and it began to rain. I take this pen. I write and write and write. This pen then becomes a sword and I strike at the page repeatedly. It has a look about it. The written work. It is dark and pleasing at the same time. It gives me pleasant thoughts at the same time I think about genocide and suicide in the same breath.
There is nothing dumb about pain. For me to exist pain has to exist. For the girl inside of me to be a late bloomer as flowers bloom in a garden, pain must also find a way out of this equation and bloom, a latecomer. We are visitors, angels with the eyes of shrouds, pain has the perspective of the next big thing, and that the show must go on. I

am never leaving. Pain and I bloom side by side elegantly do you not know it. I tell pain. You are only a piece of furniture. I tell pain. You are only a flame. Pain and romanticism are inseparable. Pain and I are husband and wife. There are great poets. There are great paintings. I think to myself if there more great men than there are great women then I must throw myself back into the great lake.

'Russia was the land that borders on God,' Rilke said.

Sardines on toast please. No sons have I although I am still a lover of other mothers' progeny. I delight in them. I have discovered I can do clever things with my hands. Artistic things. Instead of braiding hair, I can intuitively thread words. They are my fish. It is no longer winter here. I am no longer a guest in my own country. I praise your silence and the personal space. You left behind and I feel the tightness in my heart. I praise you I praise all of you but most of all I have been left behind in a tunnel into the black. There is insomnia even in a sermon and electric wavelengths in a lecture room. A female writer journaling away in her diary but where are the children and the husband. She has none. For now, she has none.

She is afraid of those words. That those words will make cell walls around her. That those words will become her prison. Winter with its shark teeth that threatens to overwhelm her every waking thought and moment. She thinks of grief and remembers her childhood and the fact that her mother never held her hand when she crossed the road or believed in her. When looking left then right what is she grieving for? What is she living for? What is she praying for? Midnight's children. Children who live under the bridge. They smoke cigarettes as if their lives depended on it. In another poem. In another lifetime, another life there was a mistake. There was a little obsession. A predestined promise of procrastination that smelled like perfume.

Then too soon, you will realise that you should not have walked away in that moment even though you were forgiven child of God. Child of an extraordinary God stripped of all illusion and fear of expectation. And as Marie Antoinette was led to a guillotine are we not all at some stage in our lives? Do we not have to live with our misgivings? And with being misrepresented, dancing around golden laughter in our mouths that we do not want to escape from. We want to search forever more for that most singular delusion swinging swiftly. I like my innocence and I like my imperfections. I like the fact that I am flawed and that I am confessing to it. Let silence speak for itself like a birthday.

Grief is only a warning. Denial too. I need to find out why the brightness dies and the flowers heads. Everyone. Every man is a machine. Every woman is a cog and a wheel in that machine. I am toxic. I am too self-conscious. I come laden with self-portraits and customs. Gaze at me and you will only see an empty look in my eyes. Vacant. Vacant. The serious depths of which have a vacant beauty. Blame me for everything. It is okay. I can take it. All toxic people are damaged or writers. They have all suffered loss. Their family life is dysfunctional. If only I could get a handle on relationships. If only they did not have a handle on me. I am in a hurry today. A release of joy in my heart. The Pulitzer. The Pulitzer.

Look at me as if I am the woman that you are coming home to in the evenings. Look at me as if I am the mother of your children pouring out your single malt whisky in your glass before you will eat the supper that I have prepared for you. This is probably what they mean by migration. What happens after the happy conclusion, after the honeymoon is it the long migration. The migration is having the progeny, the children with the angel shine on their faces, watching genocide on the news or reading about it in the paper from the perspective of a political correspondent. The migration is raising a family, growing old together but nothing was meant to be conventional in my life.

My mother never taught me what to do about the unconventional ingredients of life. I can tell you this. It will be a flawless day on which I die. Men will go into war. There will be girls and women losing their looks working in factories. Mothers and daughters side by side but I will not be one of them. On the day that I die, I will be wearing a fur coat.

Stranger made of flesh and Nineveh

Burn bright tonight tigers inside
this room. Bring me courage so
delicate. The sensation of falling. Jerusalem. Moses. Desert country.
The ancient knowledge of the importance of
family. Scarlet thread to patchwork
the burning tapestry of my soul.
I've been wounded before all of this.

I'm crying and I don't know why I'm crying.

Living with illness has done this
to me. Coming home from the sea
we have a shared interest for the
rural. Obituary. Sympathy for grassroots and
community. Proof that singing in
the rain could not dampen our spirits. Our prayer
for the eternity of the grace of the
tomorrow-land of mountain-roots.
The blue light persists. Exists only to promise
moral scorching. A wasteland of
gathering stages of spring decay and
pollen falling like dandelion clocks
all around. Such is the strange nature of illness
and the authentic mud season in the
garden. Leaves lyrical. We're the
hope. The soul on fire almost spiritual.
All I see is a field that burns me up.
Flowers survive in the moonlight.
Anointed with perfume and music schools.
After dreamy-loneliness and death comes a
world of concern. Grief brings with it

silence. Love that can move planets.
All writers are poets in their own way.
The rain saved me. It always saved
me. Breathed life back into me. I'm
only in need of a survival-kit. Little-fed
waves of afternoon sunlight. Believe
in me is all that I ask of the men and
women in my life. Fish swim towards
the nature of life. The psychological compass of its
wet valleys and runaway plankton.
Picturesque sea don't forget about me.
My strong limbs swimming against
the current. It is wild out there. A church.

Woman with the graceful neck you must love me.

The packed suitcase

Rapture is the son of Johannesburg.

The same way that Prague is
now the adopted hometown
of my sister. He did not love
me. In return, I did not love him.
He took my mother and father's
love wherever he went in the
world and everywhere I went I lived

in a self-imposed exile. People
could be kind but I only learned
that later on. In my mid-thirties.
In other words, when I was grown.
He dropped me off at the mental
institution (Tara) on a Monday morning.
Never even looked at me as if
I was a real, live person. I was
a walking experiment-in-the-making.
'Not to be touched or spoken to
if anyone could help it'. I was fresh
from a weekend spent cooking
over steaming pots, gossip with a diabetic aunt. Her youngest
daughter

tucked away safely behind a

mountain and green-lit valleys
of Swaziland. The other in America.
They could make the life choice
of being wives and mothers, (if

they wanted to). Like a river's

sublime movements, my cousin watches
me out of the corner of his eye. For any

sudden movements, I guess. I learned the hard way.
Heat rising up his neck. I learned the harsh way that

family could not be kind.
You can't sing, so you
can't fit and a family that
can't sing together can't
live together. This tiger
is not welcome, the other
tigers seem to sing in unison. I'm standing at the door of the church
hall. Waiting.
Pretending that I've been invited to the party.
That I fit in. That I can sing.

The bone slums

I think of the deepest tragedies
that I have experienced. That

have made me become the woman
that I am today. I think of Antigone,

Joan of Arc, the war of art, years
gone by. I think of death and life.
Instinct and emptiness. In the bone

slums. You will find the winter-themed of
the soul there. Stray cats. Kitchen tables that
have a rustic feel to them. Jam and bread.

Forget this place of weeping.

The preparation for a daughter to become a mother.

The yield and harvest of fathers.
The yellow star on coats.

The strange pale fire in Anne Frank's eyes.

Jewish children in the fire of war.

In the fire of the concentration camps.
I weep for nightfall. All I can do now

Is look at it from a distance. Women
Covering themselves with the veil of

justice. While men want freedom and I remember this.

That there is bitter relief to be
Found in the anguished wild.

When the final hour came, it
was a day of thunder, submission and falling.

That was the day the sun died.
That was the day the sun died.
That was the day the sun died.

And the bitter seed sung that all should
be free. That we should all be free and
hopeful. And forget the harvest of futility.

Because a ghost was in my blood

I can feel the rain even
when I close my eyes.
Taste it in my mouth. Here's the fabulous
ambitious sun. A warning to
all who dream of living
and making it good in
the big city. The land is
black at night. It haunts.
It haunts. Filled with shadows
and light and despair. I
face beating fears in the
moonlight's rural country.
The haunting abandonment of
touch scores my personality in
some indefinable way. The
discipline and source of silence
marks me like death.

Faith can break you.
Transform the fire in your heart.
The compass that I
hold in my hand helps
me navigate my passage
north. The constant heat
of the day shining for
all of its worth in all its
silken slumber. Liberty
is master. Proof is mistress.
I find pleasure in my
mother's garden. The sun glides
across my spirit. Winged sphere

and harmless burn. The sports of
earth. My grief is published here on the page.
Grief, I don't want to
forget you. Your triumph fierce. The sea is made up of
the vibrations of a
purple light. Tide and current washed
up on the shore.
You're a shadow of a
telephone pole. All things lovely beating down my door.
The foam blooms a white kind of spray.
Mankind's soul is a faithful progress.
She has a starling mouth. The lips of a mermaid.

I can still taste the rain in my mouth.

A month of Sundays and prayers

And all I can think of
is the River Ouse. Virginia Woolf's
River Ouse pouring its
distillate of salt and river into me.

The leaves are as shiny as
abalone in winter. They desire little or no sun today.
The earth's veil and garment are wet
through. No family structure of
stars, sun or moon required. The
sweetness of night falling all around
me. Such is nature. The television
said that Namibia is like a time machine.
Such is the nature of illness too. It comes
with the observations of a lifetime
gathered there. Smoke holy. Men
and women holier than thou. You can also become a
poet writing poems about nature.

And all I can think of
is the River Ouse. Virginia Woolf's
River Ouse pouring its
distillate of salt and river into me.

I want to live as near to the sea
as possible. Yes, please! So, I can wake up each morning
with my soul marked with water.
Winter comes with a map. She will
have to give of herself first to the
child before anything else. When it
cries or wants to be fed. That is if

she decides to have children one day.
She comes with a map too. I have reading
hands. Her storm river mouth is not
quite as alien to me as it once was. She's a leap of faith
that I need to take into the wild.

And all I can think of
is the River Ouse. Virginia Woolf's
River Ouse pouring its
distillate of salt and river into me.

Must travel

The day has
a moth like quality to it. I make a cup of tea (always for one).
Boil the
water in the
microwave oven while

old poems
make way for new poems. Once, I lived in grassroots country. Rural
countryside.
Mbabane, Swaziland.

(Boarding school). Slowly
my flesh is emptying out. Winter making way for spring's milky
sweetness,
summer's pleasure and
waves of heat, autumn's gift.

Slowly, I climb back
into their world. Standing in the sun sipping my cup of tea for one.
I sit and watch the
afternoon warming the page in front of me.

Gone to Jean Rhys' purple sea

Sunlight came to my house.
It came knocking. It came
and went like winter guests usually do. Like angels
or when you put away things.
The sphere of childish things.
Flowers came to my window. A
woman's reflection (or rather self-portrait).
She was standing alone in the
rain. Fading blooms on their
own out of focus journey. You're
thunder dear, I wanted to whisper
in her ear. Coming home in the
afternoon. There's a dream in
her my eyes sees. I know what
she is thinking. That this is not
the morning that she expected.
Departure. The secret of joy. Poetry in the art
of fishing. Safe footprints washed
away like yesterday. Swamp!
The depth of futility can be found there.
The almost tranquil dance of
sins and moonlight. Joyous and brave!
The sun anonymous. It flickers.
Black rain a memoir. A soul on fire and
so the change within me came.

For everything my parents taught me

Weekdays are detonated
on a Monday. Little anticipation for them at
heart. A sisterhood
of a garden of weekdays.
We weather soap operas.
The spine of the unchanging
wedding ring of the
sun. A young galaxy of
confetti with unusual
fused and acute angles.
The borrower is attractive and faithful.
The sun so political. So
trustworthy. Dripping
with personal velocity.
Mum is that faithful borrower.
She has the trustworthy
soul of a nurturer. The
invisible-like cats cling
to me. Love me until
death. The experience
of a lifetime. Starlight exhibited at peak
intervals on the shadow
of the earth. Mum's fingers
have their own calling,

Seed-thief, hollow ways
of indifference like a
thief that comes in the
night or during the day
(not on my watch). There is a volcanic
adjustment to be made

underground. The pull
of gravity. Of love. Of
life. Father gave mother
love. In return she gave me life.
The smell of gloom, of
the history of past mistakes invades
this landscape of the mother
and daughter relationship.
I know the courage of
a father. His quiet. His melancholia.
His yearning is mine and
so is his restlessness. He is
a leaf floating in history.
He is stunned with honour
and blooming power while
my mother is the cold.
She's the Pacific Ocean.

The argument

For a thousand daughters
the sun was falling. The excitement
and electric buzz of lightning.
The birds were singing. I was
arguing with my mother. I
was an adult. No longer a
child. Still wanting her love.
Her attention. Her approval.
I sucked the birth of the
machinery of the day, its sun, moon,
stardust, planets inside myself.
I looked at my beautiful and
headstrong mother and could
only see a reflection of
beautiful, headstrong me
staring back. I remained
committed to her even in
that moment. We had to
meet like this. It was fate. This rattled
my comprehension. 'Come,
sit with me. Let's talk this
out.' I wanted to say. My soul
wanted to say but didn't for
fear of losing all self-respect.

For fear of losing the
argument. I felt alive
when she said my name.
This woman had protected
me for all of my life.
Every servant has their own flame.

The argument made me
a stranger in my own home.
I don't know how it started.
Afterwards, I sat at the
kitchen table eating my
breakfast. French toast
and bacon. I relished its
greasiness. The fat on
my fingertips and lips. I eat
bacon as if it is part of
my religion. Burnt to a crisp is the
way I like it. I sweep the
saltiness, smokiness of the bacon
into my mouth regarding
the sweetness of the day.
The windows must still be washed.
The laundry must be done.

The infant

The river is filled to the bare maximum with life.
Women are more heroic than men. They have to
be. Clocks tell time. The time we must go to bed.
The time we must face another day. Smoke gets
in my brother's eyes. He opens the pathways to
the veins in my heart. I'm an animal when it comes
to books. The night is there to fill the hours with
making love. My brother is always buying cigarettes.
Bees work at night (like I do). I write poems for
a living. Work until the early hours of the morning.
My mother washes the linen. I can see the veins
on her still-life beautiful hands. When my mother
irons my brother's shirt I watch the expression
on her face. Is she happy or is she sad that he is
moving away from her in this world to the next. I
know a bird when I see them. I ask the infant,
'What is eating you?' he gurgles with delight as if
I have found his hiding place. I tell him I am going
to eat him up. His antelope legs first, his eyes, the
pink flame of his tiny hands. One day I will have
to release him. Find my exit out, hatch an escape.
One day he will be a man in a man's world and
I will be an old woman. He'll grow into fire and muscle.
I'll think to myself of the good old days when I
was young, and free to do as I please. I'll keep my
last breath a secret from the world until the end.
Until night comes and takes my aged fragility with it.

Ascension

It is a weekend of ascension and seawater.
Your face still haunts me.
She shows her face and all I see is love.
The beacon of my heart
is governed by mysterious
drowning things. Even
her laughing, serious,
fighting, sonnet movements.
Once there was an Eastern
frontier at the Eastern Cape.
A Kat River Settlement. Khoi.
Four wars were fought there
between the Xhosa and the
settlers but that's history.
Men were like twisting flame.
The sermon of the major
earth is serene now. It's a
winter sky and a winter rain
that gathers overhead from
eternity to the hereafter. The

faded call of unsung sorrow.
You mum belong to a barefoot
people. The terror of the
Pacific when it comes to your
tribe of children. You taught
me to lead and not to follow.
You were the skilled expert
when it came to my rage. I
only have to say that I am hungry
and my mother feeds her cub.

The continuous noise inside
my head goes away but not the
memory of my mother's forehead.
Her astonishingly beautiful
African violets. The scene of
luscious green grass from childhood
forgotten. Her face is still
hauntingly beautiful. You, who
taught me how to write about everything I know.
To see the world around me.

Rain

She's graceful. A wall of flame. She's beautiful.
She's the lover that I will never have. The morning
is vulnerable and open like the face of a beautiful
man who is staring at the woman he is deeply in
love with. I think of God when I think of her. Of
course, He created her. The woman that I am in
love with. There can never be anything between us.
She will go on to have fearless children. I will go
on to write novels. She is married to a poet. (All men
are poets in their own way). We haven't really
talked. She admires me in her own way and I admire
her. In photographs, her magazine-hair is wavy.
Luxurious. She looks like a film star. I want to mark

the return of the tragic hero and saint in her arms.
I want to find the peace and harmony that I cannot
find anywhere else there (in her arms). I used to
think about death but now when I see her, think of
her, all I can think of is life. I want to come just
as I am to the breathy dream of her. The goal of her.
She's savage in her love (I know) and I already
know that I won't be able to exist in that kind of world.
All my life, love and the relationships I've had
with others have been supervised. First, by my parents.
My mother's instinct. My father's inhospitable silence.
Then by a God that had to be feared. A God
that died for humankind's sins. So, I flit and

flirt from men and women powerful and elegant
in their own way. I know the world of prayer
and meditation but I don't pray to be with her.

I pray for her future happiness. I know the chaste
world of hospital corridors. That universe of
doctors and nurses and patients and medicine.
I've spent winters in hospitals (every year or
so, when the depression returns). She's changing
the world around her like a world seen
through falling snow. She is body. She is soul. I am body too. I am
soul.
All I want to do is kiss her sweet open vulnerable
face. Her moonlit shoulder blades. The nape of her milky
neck. (Of course, I know nothing will come
of this love). She will raise fearless children (that's the
reality of the situation), and I will go on to write novels.

Teaching

We never stop learning. Schools provide the base and life gives it depth. Can we ever academically learn what or how to feel?

Virginia Woolf in the Flesh

Before she began her day's, work Virginia Woolf began to write painstakingly yet in a beautiful old-fashioned script in her diary. 'Madness is not a proper sitting-down affair like a dinner or high tea. Its black wonder, in all its glorious power and kingdoms (the 'arthritic' kingdom, the 'counter-productive' kingdom, the 'body double's' kingdom), the onset and expedition into ageing, all are written on the body and in the mind of the creative.

I am placed in the centre of it. I am the key that unlocks its history. I know even when I am anxious I must be loyal to my soul's progress by letting things go. Skill comes with the potential of the 'floodgates' of each emotional curve opening up and freeing me.

Instead of hitting your head against the formidable of all formidables, the brick wall that you seem/I seem to effortlessly cling to will cave in with consummate ease and we will transcend those dazzling boundaries of what we once occupied. All I feel is winter at the back of me, draping itself like a cool shroud over me, shutting out the white light, swirls, cloud-bursts of air as heavy as moss draining me of energy, leaving me to ask myself that marked question of all marked questions, has my time come, is it my turn, is my time up? I am conscious of the time of day. It is nearly time for my afternoon walk. Faces joined to bodies hard at work in fields peer out at me with picture-perfect clarity.

I do not know them, they do not fit or belong in my world, so I go on my own merry way and pretend I do not see them. Is it nearly time for my customary nap or to have a little light supper with Leonard and talk about Hogarth Press, its cumulative progress and the writers he is currently printing?

I climb hills with style, sucked into this novel earth with each step. When I feel most not of the flesh is when a spell of madness comes upon me. All around me, the universe becomes a ghostly sphere. Stars are unfailing witnesses to the elements of my hallucinations. As I write this in relatively solitary confinement, in my room, I can see crystals of light evaporate in winter rain outside my window. Look, look, pressing with an index finger into the middle of the flushed salmon-pink of the palm of my right-hand as if I am investigating stigmata, I am living proof that even melancholy can elevate you. Why is it always the impoverished, the most vulnerable citizens of our environment, what that unflinching symbol of loss means to us, what is it about the lives of Outsiders that speak to us?

Head touching sky, feet touching ground, breathing in a lungful of the healthy countryside air (it feels as if it is sliding through me, the fruity richness of my organs, my blue veins) these are some of my most precious moments. Where would I be without you? All around me are the immortal heights of nature. To rest, I have the throne of a tree to lean against and the sky, even the scenery of the land is poetic. What would I do with jewels when today I have seen shades of the world through a pair of novel eyes? When you're older, you are more forgiving, stronger, amazed at your voluntary spontaneity to smile and engage with other 'artists' when you are at your best at public gatherings.

Is the world so full of life? Bright that it can hurt, cause you to weep, sob uncontrollably, can it draw a feint line of subterfuge between your sacred contract with your god and a most natural creative gift that is also relevant, compelling and unique? Hiking up my skirts, mud on my shoes, my hair plastered in an unladylike fashion against my forehead, enjoying exerting myself, finding pleasure in it, my limbs trembling, the 'lady of the manor', balanced yesterday precariously between the hell of mental illness and the eternal damnation of it all. With the last vestiges of my childhood all but removed, who was left to blame for my fragile state of mind. Mental illness had me once rigidly on fire and here I was a child again in my secret garden.

Walking, even if it was a width of a thread of our cottage, seemed to toughen my spirit from the inside out. I have learned to endure solitude (it has me hooked); even the silence has not lost its diamond-shine. I suffer in the silence that always seems to navigate its way to meet me in minuscule explosions in my presence and I did not presume that infertility was a fierce punishment or that it was a lesson in disguise. It was an earthquake offering me quiet torment before it became an uninvited guest sequestered to the attic. It was just a misunderstanding poured between my cells and platelets. Perhaps even the social discord of spiritual interference was melded to my bones, sinew and flesh and not just the biological.

In some ways there is still 'the subdued girl' about me, no Goth, no siren am I with flaming lips. I feel I have risen to the occasion brilliantly, as eternity has wanted me to by making a beautiful career of it. As I write these leaves are falling like pure drifts of snow and one day I know this diary will be held up for eternity, like so many others before my time, before my country, to public scrutiny. Newspaper hounds, scholars and pundits will declare 'it', my diaries and excerpts from them literature. They will say Virginia Woolf was a woman ahead of her time. If there is a worthy truth to that statement I am certain I shall not know of it in my own lifetime.'

She has always lived like this with the winters of loneliness. She called it 'perfection', 'bliss and the art of survival is found in an artist's creative expression', 'a natural habitat for a woman writing fiction', 'I am an artist and all writers are artists and all artists are writers', 'I find so many things useful in the cold comfort of my rituals before I sit down to work. The ritual of creating, of living, of the invincibility of routine and silence, that inner space that you are most conscious of'. In her mind's eyes, she tells herself to shut her eyes, to believe the voice of her alter ego and everything it is telling her. It is telling her, selling her, her invisible doppelganger's visions until she could even feel it in her heart. She was not tethered to anything in the material world. 'The only possession that I came into this world with and am leaving this world with is this physical body.' She had told her sister, Vanessa, who had been her most ardent companion during their childhood and adolescence. She lived in books and without them she would be lifeless, loveless and in their fundamental education they had given her she saw images of the wisdom she would one day come to possess.

Quiver

There are ways of diversity
made of iron when it comes
to gender. The opposite sex.
The female gender. The song of
the feminine. Children under
the age of eight love my mother.
They adore her glowing red
lips. Her magazine hair and
fashion. My father brought
both a manic utopia and his bipolar life
with him. The apocalypse.
Wherever he went I followed.
The dutiful little schoolgirl.
I was always a little bit in awe of him.
His high mountains. Complex rivers.
The pastures found in valleys.
I still am. She's giving him

the silent treatment. She's screaming at him at the

top of her lungs. She called
him a homosexual but what's
so bad about that except he's

her husband. The father of her
three children. She cannot
bear to let him touch her so they
sleep in separate beds but in
the. same room. It's a bit like
living on an island surrounded

by applause. So, in return her children scream at her.

Shut her out of their lives
but at the same time, they cling to
their mother's apron strings
because she is all that they know
of mother love. Documentaries
taught them about the assassinated
writer and academic Rick Turner.
The assassinated communist leader
Chris Hani. The great leader

Patrice Lumumba and the
celebrated poet Maya Angelou. If my mother
had loved me perhaps I would
have been a different person. So, I write to silence
the pain of the false illusion.
The arrows are the gift. The
reward at the end of the day's hours.

Daughters and their fathers

I brew tea, magic spells inside a
pot while dad listens to Mozart.
In polaroid heaven, wet hair clings
to my neck. I'm thinking of going
into therapy again in my late thirties.
I circle the box of cold pizza.
Put the kettle on again because it
gives me something to do. Something
to pass the time. The salt and
brilliant light of the hours. I think
of the ghost of the day. The darkness
that night yields. The bird (a
gull or swallow) as it coasts through
the air. I stare at the fable of
daughters and their fathers unfolding
in front of me, forgetting (yes, yea,
forgetting) that I am not black.
Forgetting that racist comment
made by someone like me. Think of
the woven vision in the earthquake
inside of me. I'm one of them and
perhaps so are you. One of those tragic
creatures who can pass for white.
And I think of my lover's hands.
My lover's sensitive hands. How shattered
and wounded I felt in his presence,
when he didn't say I love you back.
He was the sun, moon and stars,
my scars and sorrows, my morning tonic.
Now he's working in film. I remember
how he took me out for coffee once, talking,

talking, talking to New York people. I wonder if

he still lives in Johannesburg. Maybe
he's married now. Maybe he's happy.
I want to be loved. I want those reading

hands. I want the lion instinct of
mystery and mysticism. Solitude has
even found a way into my bloodstream.

The darkness came with my father.
So, did the bone museum. Museums
and women. Men named Gus and Hugh.

They taught me how to brave courage
and sky. November looks pale.
I think of the brilliant dead. I think of

the brilliant living. That dark
light that dares to linger. I think of nightfall.
Mothers and daughters in orbit.

Grief for my second mother. Grief for
the woman that I've now become.
The good one who stayed put to

look after her elderly father. Who gave up
her life. She's got the tickets to
a lost country but nobody ever speaks of that.

A Woman at Work

In my winter's night
of dreams and visions,
you're there. I find
myself in the interiors
of a museum. With love,
here are dahlias in my
hands. Do you accept it
or refuse it? When daylight falls
lonely I find I have a lost
ghost of a soul. All these
years I have lived a secret
life and inside the painted
blue you will find the hidden. The electric.
The mountain and the
field's spark. There was
some sadness behind her
smile, her eyes. The speed
of darkness too. I know you.
I wanted to tell her. I've
been where you are. My
mother, my father's wife.
When love speaks it brings
with it our dreams. Pure

and healthy as water. To us
it speaks about Paris. When
love speaks to me there's a
story behind the poem. The
poetry experiment. It speaks
to me about the emptiness and grief
before it speaks to me about

a portrait of a child or the sun.
Older. Further. Beyond. The
discovery of it a thousand times
in a day. Bodies and limbs made
out of sunlight. This woman's
work saves autumn. The ethereal
of the monster abundance
of that season's change in
the air. The harshness. The
struggle-ish. The gratitude of
the narrator. Here comes the
remainder of the blemished sun craving
Noah's ark and his animals.
More, more. The quiet sea says to
the coast. I want more of you.

The red-sparrow instinct of the phoenix

The wild can be savage. Forgive me.
Forgive me. It is my lack of memory.
The night. The night. Ghosts falling
from the attic of my soul. Your mouth.
Your eyes. You're near and that is all
that matters. Linger. Linger. Frame
the depths of your heart. Sacrifice your
heart in your twenties. Give up those
ghosts but only if you want to. Only
if you dare. Look at this verse. Read
this and weep or laugh because this
is cupid-country. I only knew of liberty
when you left you see. There was no
other way to print the face of God on the grass that
just grows and birds that just fly away. A woman
loved is changed. I'm in the deep end
of the swimming pool again. A mermaid
numb to the bone with desire and winter-
mischief. I'm a hungry and thirsty traveller
with my head in the kingdom of clouds.
A tangled mermaid. Half-fish. Half-bone.

Half-flesh not tasting of smoke or plume.
I have few excellent friends that I write to.
It is the writing that is the great unknown. The song.
The pizza is cold but I eat it anyway.
Even depressed I would pray. Meditate.
Sit in silence for hours on end in my
bedroom, and the wound would become
a spell. The hospital bed would become
the source of that spell. I was sad then happy

then sad again but all this time I could
still write. I wrote for my Father who art
in heaven and my biological father. I
wrote for my brother, and his son. My
mother and my sister. Your poetry is
made of concrete though. You're priest,
and curator. Prophet and husband. Father
and poet. You're brilliant with words, Joop
Bersee. I'm writing this for you. To you. Eating this
cold pizza was as depressing as the day.
Near the city of Johannesburg there's a
darkness there that's the friend of sinners.

As I stand in this empty space

Only to write. Only this lonely existence
keeping me alive. Living far-off. Living
distant. We must make up for wasting life.
What I've discovered near to the city of
Johannesburg is this house of the good sun.
Branches with their own mother tongue.
Even shadows have dreams. Even they forget
time. Wives contemplate the lives of
their children in the park, or the man who
cannot take his eyes off of them. I think of
my exit to Johannesburg. Old magazines
that I pack away alongside newspapers with
my photograph in them. I tell myself that
I am woman. I am woman. Study me.
Observe me. Dance with me. Come sit

with me at the fire, where the earth turns
black underneath. I'd like you to come
to my house and see how I live now. How
I live without you. Without love. Without
the bondage of that seed, and the fact that there's
no harvest that comes with damaged people.
I think of Diane Arbus, Susan Sontag. Anna
Akhmatova and Osip Mandelstam. Genna
Gardini and James Dean and Robert Lowell.
I think of our brief relationship buried in
dust, in rehab, in another world's earth, and
I think of rituals. Tiny, and perfect, and pure.
because this is where I am now. Hearing
voices from the distant past, or only from a
few hours ago. You're just a binary star.

Through the rain there's a closing door.
With the flow of dark-green water over my shoulder
blades, and I think to myself what song
took you to the dance-floor of your wedding.
I think of the woman who is now your wife.
Her hand in yours. Trusting you in the same
way I trusted you. I want you to take me into
your silence. There was man. A bone-thin
woman with blue wrists. Death, only death
can hold you now, because here, yes, here in this
ocean I have no dream-husband of my own.

To the resting place of the light house

You've withdrawn from me with your half-
closed eyes ragdoll child. You have the
winter chill inside of you. I am many things.
Sad and intellectual. Wounded animal and
the greenness of a mountain. Your mouth
is a dream, and a spring. Water and smoke
painted inside the weather-body of my winter.
My mind's eye. You're my brave new world.
My progress lost in translation. I dream of
fireworks in this house full of women who
are daughters. I drink my coffee to the background
noise of birdsong and morning traffic scattered throughout
in suburbia. Mum is nature's bride. The only
woman who was ever a bride in the house.
It was my sister who taught me that shoes
have a supporting role to play in life. I've known
low spirits and sunshine. Storms and music.
I've dreamed through the visions of Jean Rhys'
life. I've been under and above. My aura is
my education. I've called that life-teacher, wise-
master of philosophy. I am glory and bright-
tiger. Animals inspire me. Some days I'm
giving. Some days I'm sad. Some days have
too much winter in them. The pizza is cold
but my body still craves it. One day the world
will go on as if I never existed but I'm not
frightened of that tomorrow anymore. This
house filled with infinite rainforest and drowning
people, plants that look like trees, a kitchen
that's an island, rooms that I have to make
pilgrimages across. And the ceiling above my

head are filled with birds. When I shower I
can hear birdsong in this madness palace.
I drink rose petal and vanilla tea with the morning
newspapers. I think of the wrinkles, the
fine lines around my mouth and eyes that
I am discovering now for the first time. The
white hairs on my head. Call it wisdom then
if you want to. Here is the dream-husband.
He appears in shadow. In the making of self,
and my ego, and identity as writer. There
are roots, and unfinished desire. There are goals, and Biko,
and Fanon's wretchedness to write about.

When the philosopher came into my life

You don't know my moth sorrows. The

challenges of finding love. She only
telephones to speak to mother. All
her life she's been searching for love.
She wants to be in the family way. It
doesn't matter to her if it is a son or a
daughter. She's searching for everything.
For happiness. For the supernatural in
everything. And so, what do you see
when you see me. She can eat her dinner
in a fancy restaurant if she wants. Over
the years I've learned the discipline
that comes with the terrifying quiet. I've
lost myself in Merchant Ivory films.
The spiritual warfare of art. The deep bonds
of family. In the mornings I think of
the breakfasts I had as a small child.
Food and coffee. Toast and muesli with yogurt.
She came into my life with her winter
Aura. Her sun in my face. Wildflowers
all around me. The smell of her perfume.
Love is as ancient as rain. The prophets.

You don't know anything about the smoke
in my lungs. My mother was this perfect
courageous being. I want to listen to her
laughing eyes for the rest of my life.
There was a sane life, an insane life, and
a reality that was both a curse and a gift.
I've been burdened my entire life by some

some past regret. Some past indiscretion.

Nobody remembers Majdanek. They
remember the word holocaust. Auschwitz.
The concentration camps. Noah had a rapid
fire journey into the unknown high seas.
This, this is my soul. She's coming home
for the long weekend. We're all outside in
the backyard in our own worlds. I don't
want to go inside yet. I haven't had enough

sun. I think of her face. A face I've come to
know so well. I think of the future lines on
my sister's face. I think of her loving man,
woman and child. Daughter or son. Sons and
Daughters. Transformed by fire, by tigers,
by golden flame. I think of her future soul.
It is the wise woman that has the prophetic
voice, and I think to myself that if she

promises me the manifesto of her heart,
I will tell her all my Plathian-secrets. She's
done the impossible. She's free. She's free.
I think of ceremonial bodies. Governing
bodies. The earthly plane, heaven, paradise,
the careful shattering of all-consequence
when love comes to an end. I think of the
harvest-time of the kingdom of blood that
flows through my veins, the root of cell
and platelet that hides itself away. Most of
all I think of the third eye. How we're all
connected. Mankind. Soul to soul to the
subtle qualities of spirituality and I think of how

I want nothing in this world to harm her.

Just looking for a place to rest my head

I remember being asked about the two-faced
dilemma of the light of the day. What it felt like.
I remembered the rain, thought of the abandoned
journeys of my life, driftwood, ocean, river as
it flows into ocean. When I think of you I think
of walls of stone now. The tribal song of humanity.
The crashing waves of the roaring sea. You're folly,
my atlas. My comforting progress. The little town
where I live now lapping, licking salt at the wings of my soul
and I managed loss brick-by-brick. Thinking of the
subtleties of romantic love. Standing at the water's
edge making observation after observation half-
frozen by the day. The chill in the air. Once I was
obsessed with you held back by nothing but a
thread of sanity. I swim to reach you. Only to reach
you. My personal space is awash with heat, eddies
of dust and whirlpools of stars. I'm imprisoned by
something that I cannot put into words yet. Abandoned
by your hands I am slowly going mad. Part despair. Part
the Thursday afternoon that I found myself writing
this poem. I like you. I like you just the way you are.
To the drowned throne room slowly going mad in
sickness and in health. This is a love story. Part
solitude. Part loneliness. Let me go back. I keep forgetting
that this is a love story. You with the sad eyes,
I'm only brave for you. You make me feel safe.

She listens to cool music. I prefer classical music.
Opera. Mozart. Bach. She knows more about the
world than I do. Pick madness if you must. In my
house nothing else matters. I move through the
air floating from lunatic to socialite. I sleep alone.
I have no lovers. I wake up when the birds sing.
I remember your blue shirt. I remember your blue jeans.
Once you were perfect, love but I do not exist in your
field of dreams anymore, lover. These days I lose
myself in museums and art, books, music, the radio,
watching documentaries. I think of you by my side.
Those good days. I'm sure of one thing. My proper
English. That death will come for all of us. I think
of writing into the energy of the night, the silent and
holy and sacred and lonely night that is forever holding
me hostage. You're part of the greater good again
for now. The sharks in the early, early, early morning.

Things you need to know about stardust

Open the door and you will find a kingdom

there. There are things that you need to
know about me. I have a conversation
inside my head about how some people
should not be parents but they are. But
they are. They fight in front of their children.
They watch the news or inappropriate
films. I look at my mother's bent head
over her work. I am doing this for her
but she does not notice. Does not say
anything. I look at her bird nose and her
beak mouth and I have this urge to connect
with her but she does not want to connect
with me. I feel tribal towards her. She's
an orphan in the world now. I dreamt about
my grandfather last night or was it last
week. I think of the pale fire of the sea

that resonates within me like thunder. Of
course, I have always wanted music in
my life. People are writing about modern
loss now. Living in loops. I look at my
mother's bare neck. Her shoulder blades,
and I think to myself that I came from
that. I came from her intense psychologies.
There's the upward push of her fingers
as she works. I would have put music on
or the radio but she said that she works
better in silence. She works barefoot like a
girl, and I think of her pressing into my

father's back at night when they sleep together in the
same bed, and I think of how some people
should never have been parents and then

I think of mine. I think of the silence in their bedroom and

the last things they say to each other before
putting out the light and putting their heads
on the pillow. I wonder did my father
always make my mother feel safe. I don't
know what that's like. Believing in a man.
Believing that he can give you the world.
I think of the truth about loneliness. About
how it's all stardust, moonlight and roses.
I think of the men who have been kind to
my mother in her life because she was a
beautiful woman and didn't have to work
hard for attention from kind or unkind men.
The way that I have had to work hard for
it my entire life, and I wonder if my mother
has ever kissed my father's neck like I kissed
the last man that I was ever in love with.

Karma

My entire beautiful, university-educated, elegantly-put-together mother has to her credit that she carried the three of us in her womb for nine months and that she wanted a fourth child.

Assia Wevill

Journal entry

In these early days Assia Wevill needs proof.

Will a village life be enough for us? I am planting the unsaid. The ground, the earth is fertile for the unsaid. I am planting my future delight, my afternoon delight. I am trembling healer. There is no childhood for me anymore. Tell me a story Ted Hughes. Write me a poem. It does not have to be romantic. Gaze at me. I will watch you while you sleep, while you work. Smile but to smile it has become an issue between us like malignant syrup. We are not just a marriage of two likeminded individuals but two souls. I cannot change what does not move me, what I do not desire, what I do not need. I am your apprentice and you are the master of this household who lifts the veil of my great loneliness, my attractive mask, my costume. I know that you think of my image as sensual. I cannot give that up. I too have a place in this world. Pull up a chair, sit at my kitchen table, and eat. Eat this German Jewess's food, her recipe for seeds and shoots and wings and things. Eat my chicken. Drink from the glass of water I bring you now. I feel useful now. If you want me to peel the potatoes, then I will peel the potatoes.

More killing. It is a mystery. Love is like that. Pure with all of its rituals it holds us in a death-grip and I warm to it, my heart warms to it, warms to you Ted. I am blinded by love, by my passionate rival, my nemesis, her unreason. Gaze at me, I am all starry-eyed. I am all yours. When I fall asleep you are there, when I wake you are there, articulate you and I know we are coming to the edge of a precipice when decisions, hardened choices will have to be made. I know you will leave your Sylvia. I know we will go to Spain. This is inevitable.

We will both say goodbye to her echo. The echo of the past, the echo of adultery.

Sylvia is just a dead spot now, but who knew that she would shortly become a stain multiplying, multiplying, and multiplying like rain. I am farming, and you are a nomad. I will prepare the house for us to live in, look after the children, cook, clean, prepare the meals, set the table with the proper shiny knives, forks and glasses feed the children, teach them German, play with them as if they were my own. You are my dream. I am your dream. In your own words, 'I am and always will be your exotic Assia.' We will prosper. We will build gods in this ghost house, little Buddha's, with fragrant oil on our hands we will burn sticks of incense; their perfume will fill the room. I will not harm you.

There will be wild Saturday nights, encounters with other poets and their wives, who will you fall in love with next, who will be your next dream. Know this. If I cannot triumph, I will not be able to endure.
You will take me in your arms repeatedly and again when our love is at the wuthering heights of its purest intensity. You will pin me down. You will hold me. I will pin your down. We will laugh. I do not know yet that one day my soul will be dead and you, dear Ted, you the one I love the most in the world, hold dearest will be the cause of it.

We will hold hands. We will go into the woods like children with our blanket and our picnic basket of sandwiches. You will come to me with wildflowers in your hands.

I am half-in-love. You have saved me. You have rescued me from a life half-lived, from Nazi-Germany. I think of our children in school, while they lay sleeping in their beds, half-dreaming, protected against the-evils-of-human-nature. Nobody knew what anorexia was, what anorexia nervosa, an eating disorder was. They did not know what to call it then.

My mother was my father's first lover. But I come to you with regret, lovers past and present, three husbands, discontent but clothed or even in my nakedness you can see the real me. Was I promiscuous? I do not know what the meaning of that word is. When men sleep with women are they promiscuous? When they take a woman to bed, do they feel pity, self-pity, no, little or low self-esteem or anguish? All they feel is the sexual impulse. I am the woman who is made of a much harder substance. To be significant is difficult. You are the most significant person that I know, the most famous person that I know of Ted Hughes. My Ted, my Ted, my glorious and infallible Ted. In childhood, my innocence went kaput.

Do not even look at me I should have said now when I think about it in retrospect. Do not tell me how sorry you are. You are evil. You are pure evil is what you are. Do not touch me. I know you have been with someone else. I know you have been with another one, another woman. Another one got in the way. Did you touch her the way your touched me? Do you even know what the word intimacy means? Coward! Fool! Cad or do you prefer scoundrel, rat! Get out! Do you even know what those words mean cheat? I carried two babies for you, aborted one but you felt nothing.

The first time I ever slept with a man it was tantamount to rape. I never told this to anyone. Men were rough creatures and that is a truth, not gentle, not nurturing, and not giving, oh they were gentle and nurturing enough and giving to their children, to the light of their world but not to the unseen. I always thought of violence as being something external, something outside of myself not something that I would have to live with, that would enter me, something that I would have to accept if I wanted to have the most serious love of my life in my life. The brilliant and most accomplished poet of his generation Ted Hughes. I try to remember our conversations word for word and I write it down and read it repeatedly. The goal is to get married. The goal is to get married and live happily ever after and see the brightness in his eyes and read his work (replace Sylvia). I am getting older. I am getting fatter. I am losing my allure and one day, one terrible day I believe he will leave me for someone else. He will cheat on me. I write to my sister because I cannot take any of this anymore. The isolation and the fact that everyone thinks I am an interloper. Sylvia was not a martyr. Ted is not the villain as he is made out to be. Women cannot leave him alone. They want to be around him all the time.

A drought of words in a journal

There was a home and a family that belonged
to her. Fragments in a diary. You've revealed
your true self to me and now I must do the
same. The mysteries of my sorrows are like a
constellation beyond the trees. Emptiness lingers
here. It will be hours until I sleep. And when
that fire comes I will dream under nightfall.
A million stars. It will be a quiet victory in the
morning hours. I search for the familiar in progeny.
Old photographs pasted in wedding albums. I
find myself there as I pick up this pen and begin
to write. While watching the first snow I think of
mum who believed (in me). Sacrifice. To be good
at sacrifice, falling, falling in love, worship, praise,
solitude, standing, spontaneity. Not taking the
spiritual flame for granted. That the knowledge of
stems and atoms could accomplish anything. All
artists are part of a community. Light in the darkness
come to me now. Every tear, that had to fall. The
arrows are the reward. Tears were worth the
sacrifice in the end. Fire of my soul. The fire
and volcano of my soul. The gnarled oak of my soul
adopted by a pale fire-woman and bittersweet
day and night. When she wanted alone-time she
left the child with us. I played mother. Even when he
was an infant, I played mother. She inhabits a world
I do not know or understand. The world of wife and mother.
The soul-champagne world of mother and lover.

Behold the glory of the river

I know this country. His country. Once it was

mine to hold. A gathering-wrangling crestfallen
miniature world of longing. Dying to belong
to modern society. The familiar cells of sacrifice
are there underground. There's no sun here but
it's still hot. There was a time when I was spirit.
Increasingly occupied with fear. The sky is blue
and the grass green and I think to myself that is
all I know for certain. I plant a seed and enjoy
learning it is love that changes everything. I bury
the majestic sun in the ground. In earth that was
once upon a time ago part of a volcano. Do the
same with winter. I score a congregation of birds
in watercolour. I note that this path leads to a soul's enlightenment.
The sea mocks me with a kind of thy will be done.
Dear sweet child of mine with a Jesus shine
on your face. With your big voice that drowns
out everything in my world. Your step like a
current, ancient and sure. I watch you carefully.
Melting. With a flash in my heart. Rapture in
my soul. You're a phantom landscape. You're
cinema. Manna. Honey. Milk-fed. I kiss your
cheek. The bridge of happiness-joy-peace rolling
in my lungs. When you sit on my lap I stroke your
tiger balm neck, arms, legs, back. You summon
me with exulting stare. In sleep, I watch over
you and melt. You laugh. I cling to your strong
personality. I am envious of your milk-fed fangs.
Your tales. Ether. Content, cow-boy. The gap
of your watchful heaven. Bones of your evening

paradise. Your perfect fighting city and when
the gulf of silence greets your tired sweet face and
you wrap yourself in toy, animation and sleep you
make me forget my selfish amorphous failing, painted
muffling, blind cave of grief with your solemn dance.
You make me forget that I am not good all the time. The peril of
ego and flattery. And a valley is formed in my soul.

Winter leaf and the smell of apples

I prefer being the madwoman
in the attic. A Mrs Rochester.
This happy daughter of manic-depressive George.
I understand that kind of life.
It pleases me. I can't turn my
back on it. Walk away from it.
I've already forgiven you. It's
my thing. This a modern way
of thinking on blue days. When the happy flame of
my soul is on fire. And fasting
the inner music of my soul, the
night away and old world nostalgia.
You were the one (big magic).
You're still young at heart. Your hands
are still beautiful, my consolation.
Years of silence has crept up
on both of us. Made a martyr

out of me and a saint out
of you. The big magic of solitude and loneliness
has climbed into our souls.
You're as radiant as the sun.
The same sun that makes 'climbing trees'
out of all of us. After all this
time you're still 'the one' to
me but you're married now.
You've put down ancient and
green roots in another city
that might as well be another
country. The happy dream of you

is still in my eyes. Life is hard
for me now and I wonder if you
can understand that. That my
silence is golden. My speech is silver
like the centre of winter's flux.

Tenderness and extraordinary vertigo

She reminds me of wild grass.
They remind me of wild grass.
Bone against bone. Flesh of
my flesh a prize. From all of
this reeling emptiness. Whispers of
silence and loneliness in the
afternoon sunlight. Take me
away from the nationality of
this madness. I can see it when I look into their eyes.
What exactly they think of me.
There are so many levels of
madness in my family. An obsessive,
compulsive madness about
cleanliness. Disorder. Bipolar.
Substance abuse. I could say
my mother never loved me but all
my life she was my shelter.
My teacher. My driftwood,
my potential, the windows to
my soul. My Ingrid Jonker.
My Marilyn Monroe. Been a disgrace
all my life, my mother said to
my face. Still, the wild grass comes to me.
Like the magical and intelligent films of
Stanley Kubrick. Jane Campion.
My Ingrid Jonker. My Marilyn Monroe.
Red furious hearts beating away.
Red little beasts. Wounded beasts. But also, blue and hurt and ill and
feeling wounded. I want to be free

and pain-less. I want freedom.
Inside I feel an abundant hurt.
The pain of this everlasting. Still
I feel this emptiness inside of
me. Can't put it into words. Don't
think I'm trying hard enough.
I'm feeling blue and cynical.
My heart is worn out. Out of
loving people who do not want to
love me in return. My heart is

cold. Don't tell the snow witch.
Can't fight this. Not so tough after all.

Don't have that instinct. This is
breaking my heart. Breaking the hurt

I've carried inside of me, my womb
for months. I want to tell people.

All I have ever wanted is to be loved.

Shelter and protection

I think I've changed people's minds
and a few hearts along the way but
of course, mum doesn't see it that way. All she can see is this.
That I haven't lived up to my full
potential. That I am not as beautiful
as my sister who always comes up smelling of roses. So, I take the hurt
and mend it. Call the threads of
it enigmatic and prize-giving. I've wanted
love all my life. Never been greedy
enough to take it for myself. I've
been lonely. Wandered through this
life careless. Made mistakes. (Have been unhappy.)
Frightened that I'd live life that way
forever and end up with revenge in
my heart. All I've ever wanted is love.
This is breaking my heart. Can you
see that it is breaking my heart with
every word that I write this. As the
afternoon sun sets I want to tell people.
Don't take the emptiness. Don't let
futility rule your life. Don't let loneliness overwhelm
you at the worst of times. I look at
my mother's face and all I can see is
her tired, sad yet pretty face. I look
at my father. The exposure of time in the lines and wrinkles
and all I can see is this. Me ending
up like him. Obsessive. Overly sensitive.
Bipolar and weak. Drinking cold
coffee with a cat on my lap. Left
out in the cold tasting solitude barefoot.

Drifting. Cast out into a pink-salmon
world where paradise and heaven
can never survive. I think of the sea and
place. The lightning and thunder
of the sea on a hot day ruled by Alanis Morrissette

and the Irish band Ash. You're
electricity, physics, chemistry. Survival.
Instinct. Biological. Environmental.
Your memory is vapour. A field
with layers of snow. You're frost.
Veins filled with ice water. I've
gone swimming in my imagination again.

Away from you this time. I feel
endangered like the all the polluted rivers of South Africa.
Up close what do you see, think,
feel about me. This is when love is not enough.
When all that life signals is rain.

Look out or burn! There's a moth
storm transfer of energy that is
wasteland wilderness a-coming
on a mountain. In place, seams gathering
of blue light a swarm of place
and tide and current. Dark wavelengths
of inspired-magazine hair. Coming
home from the sea there's a window that's open
somewhere. A chill in the air. A draft.

I have to close it for the rain. And
as long as writing restores me to
sanity I will keep living towards the light of

doing good. I can't love you. It is
not in me to love you. Forgive me. Letting it

burn in the end will cost me everything.

Hive

Stability sometimes has to make
room for hunger. The spoils of
war. Harvest sometimes has to
make room for another harvest
in spring. The beating heart sometimes has
to make room for another heart.
The ripe suns in this galaxy and
beyond have their own sense of urgency wasting away.
Dementia is found there in the air.
Its clarity is specific. It has the concentration
of the perfect image in focus.

The spool under a wishful current.
(of a poet-writer battling depression,
battling on to find sanity but no one
speaks of this anymore). To begin with, you flew away.
Your charm scientific. Your heart is

factual. You taught me that. The river falls.

You fall. A waterfall in your eyes.
Determined hush falls all around.
The pool is logical but also sinister.
Originally it was wild there and found in a
rural kingdom cometh. The soul
cannot change. Cannot dream. Cannot sustain itself
without the hive. The swarm in
union and within their solidarity

comes the wounded. An ill feeling of hurt
as dark as sea. I take the stitches

of this ballroom masquerade party
inside out. I don't want to listen to
this. Hearing my parents argue into
the night. I follow the vibrations of
the news scribbling across the TV
screen. I don't want your glitter. I
don't want your pain, empty vessel.

Even ripe flowers find a way to exist.
Pollen and tension have a history that
chases down aural pathways in ancient history.
You were unkind. You did not write
or call when he went to rehab. I felt
I could not dream, not sleep anymore.
Had to take the appropriate pill to cure me.
In order not to pursue a road to madness.

The painted birds

I'm helpless. She knows this and tells me
to forget this place of weeping and change.
She's an afternoon shadow. A crack in the
wall. A crack in the system. She doesn't
believe in the Holy Spirit. Once she was
a daughter. Now she is a lover. She's the
opposite of me. She's beautiful and caring

to those who know her well. I don't know
anyone. I don't know people. All I know of
is poverty. The heavenly peace of religious order. Instead,
I know the powerful language of the birds.
Films. Susan Sontag and Wuthering Heights.
But she doesn't understand this. Why I
Shake like a fish in danger from being swept
from the sea. The fish a hero for service.
I know the passages of grief. Those trespassed floodgates.
I've bathed in the Rome of grief. The happy
joys of soon to be forgotten pasta. Wine.

I've painted pictures of a mad country in words.
That's my truth. That's the currency I deal in.
It is also my sadness. My madness is my sadness.
All my life I've searched for a cure. Never
coming close. Only to demise and despair.
I would have offered my whole life to the supernatural
if the madness stopped. Conversation with
nails made of flame made of the master of nightmares.
Anything to stop the drowning. That fear.

Instead, I have always been the author.

The poet, and my struggles have been
both public and private. I've searched
place and time and space. Holistic and the personal.

The history of this has always been
sacred and as cold as winter. Just as
powerful and present. Burning fire in my hands.
Adored and not wanted. Adored and
not wanted. Similes and metaphors.
They judge. Judge me. Tie me up and down.
High and low. I always have to take
its temperature. Follow in its footsteps.

Its noise leaves the cells of my heart
vulnerable. The door to my soul opens wide.
My eyes wise to its repeated progress.

All about Eve

On this brilliant summer day let's do

away with instinct, Moses, Joan of Arc,
Albert Schweitzer, Franz Kafka, and
Emily Dickinson and return to words,
the nature of life, the birth of morning
inheriting the wolf. I do not want to
live here forever like this. Finding the
source of Everest, the Nile. I study her.
Her hair, her belly, her smile, her laughter.
Her beautiful, and sensitive hands and
interesting face. The one I call mother.
Triumph and hope, despair and triumph
co-exist. The lover becomes philosopher, I
become teacher. I think of her red shoes,
the ex. My brother's ex and of how
she's no longer here in this space. I
think of the happy vibes between lovers,

cold sunlight, the life of the sea, the
swimming pool. I'm wounded looking
out at the veil of this coastal city. Waves
flood every nerve. My anxiety withers
in this storm. This, this is my story. The door
appeared like dark paper. The craft of
writing, for example, brings me to you.
The Johannesburg of you. I think of the
radio playing in my lungs. Mountains on
the television. I listen to the social outcast
eating dry bread and who wants to
make a conversation with me. I think

of the icy mouth of winter's stamina.
You're begging for another survival-
cycle, lover. My hands. Yes, these hands
carry this human stain. This is not goodbye,
and I will fear no evil. I'll only live
for the greater good. Be a man. Go on!
Be a man. The reward will be freedom.

All my life Rilke in my hands

Leaves become branches, tracks, reaching
towards the sky. I surrender but still tell the city to
remain close. To the aroma of grief. I follow
her down the mountain, and through the dry
grass of the valley. Her flesh is a prize. Look
at the poor, those who live in poverty. On the
day we fell in love with words we didn't see them. Look
at those who suffer hardship after hardship.
Love leaves me with the dead greats, so does
loss. I think of philosophy and literature in
the same breath. You're as relevant as climate
change, and global warming. She's truly an
amazing thing. Desolate, and charming. Vivacious
too! One day she'll be taken away from me.
She'll become like a Jupiter's moon then. She'll finally
 live in eternity. All my life I've lived in the
world of the flesh like a bird with a broken
wing. Her stories are like rubies to me when
I'm lost and scared, and the hours are strange when
I'm not writing. When all I have are tears crawling
on the flesh of my skin. This, this writing that
is in my blood like the wild birds of Kenya.
Her blood brings me warmth, originality, an

authenticity. She has stopped writing, but there's
still salt in the ocean. The summer rain still
falls. It is still hard to say sorry I broke your
heart. I made a mistake loving you. Don't be
afraid, I want to tell her, but I'm afraid too. Afraid
of dying young. Dying too young, or living
until I am too frail to love this world, this earth

anymore. I still want to be left alone. I wrote
this for you gifted daughter of Kenya. On her
farm she is hunter and gatherer. I think of the
passing of Sam Nzima, the worship of the ancestors,
her suffering, my loss, Africa's loss, everything
within me, the word uhuru, the shape of winter
in the ground. I think of the soil that she ploughs.
I think of water, her aura, her soul, my soul.
The protest that both loneliness and silence in all
of these hours' witnesses. I sit and wait. I sit

and wait for the light. I want to look at the ocean
in this light. I think of how she doesn't have
the time to write anymore. She's the land of glory
but doesn't know it. I think of refugees. I think
of Cuba. Cities are selfish. They take and take
and take. Leave us with a difficult exhale, circles
in difficult arguments, falling, devastation and
collapse when we cannot write. When we cannot
put those words down on the page. When the pen
is not mightier than the sword. I think of how vast
her throat is. The sadness is gone now. The regret.
All I see is a metamorphosis. Her face a flower, and I see
how her philosophy finds shelter here inside of me.

In expectation of you showing up

You're water
(you've drowned my soul)
You're a shroud
(you've covered me with the sweetness of kisses
that taste like sugar)
You're healing
(a museum)
You're a spark
(you're sweat, tears)
You're profound
(you're the history of hours past, present, future)
Has anyone ever
told you that or
written you a
poem, a love poem
to celebrate who
you are gloriously.
You're water
(you're pure)
You're a compass facing the end of the world
I know it that feeling well
(you're found in the
glamorous wild)
You're from the stars
(made of that matter,
ice, lungs, lukewarm
mugs of herbal tea).
You're gone but
sometimes I think
you're still here.
That if I turn my head

you'll be in the kitchen
preparing sardines
on toast for us
or you're lying on your
half of the bed in our
shared bedroom resting.

The nature of things

The nature of things may be different to every person. I do not know. All I know is my interpretation.

The Split Personalities of Elizabeth Donkin

I had a wood when I was a child. There was a forest near my childhood home. At night, before I would blow my lamp out I would stare out into that darkness that seemed to be stalking me. Forever stalking me, do you understand? It would suit my mood and I would will myself not to dream. To summon angels instead to surround my bed so I would not have bad dreams, does that make any sense to you? I would find myself in a field surrounded by farmers ploughing it. Totally ignoring me. A little girl. An English girl who would grow up to be a lady. I would not play with my boy cousins. They were too rough. My husband, my husband understands me gloriously, ingloriously. He makes me feel as if I am a real person. He is an Elijah. I would have cool thoughts when I was a child. Then the morning sun would delicately ripen everything inside my childhood bedroom. Soft, sweet gentle light. How I long for you and nurse? How I long for my nursery and for nursery food?

I am greedy for the flame of life in the veins of my physical body. I am in my quarters again. Rufane kissed me chastely. He kissed my forehead, my wrists and then I was in a trance, said I was so pale, asked me did I have anything to eat. He is like a child always wanting my attention, my approval for everything. I am a wife, so I must give in and when he leaves me I am quite alone with my thoughts and I can already feel the heat, the genuine warmth of Africa rising in my blood. It is wonderful. Beautiful like ash settling on the ground after a bonfire and the air still warm after the fire has died down. This warmth, it is spreading throughout my body, my arms, my shoulders, my knees, legs and the chambers of my heart. It is a physical assault. It is a sacrifice on my part. I feel a burning sensation now when I have written down too much of the spasms that go throughout my body. Stress, the doctor said. Nothing to worry too much about. Nothing that travelling to a new world cannot cure.

Halt! I cannot stand the smell of this fish pie even though it reminds me of home. Now watch your salt intake. The doctor said not too little of this, not too much of that. Poor fish. Served up as grub for me. Their tails so innocent. I can imagine them flapping in water. Gills in need of air, nothing to quieten down that thirst. I need to eat. I know that, and I feel so weak if I do not put anything past my lips but the food tastes bland. There is a fury in me when I feel so weak. I know I have faults and weaknesses now. I have limits, but I do not think my poor, longsuffering husband can understand this. As a wife now, I have limits. When he burns my skin that fabric, and that tapestry ever so gently I think he needs to be reminded of that fact. Not of my innocence but of my own self-control. He talks of my radiance when he is in that mood. He talks of my secret beauty. He talks of his guilt too of taking me away from the only home I have ever known but he also talks of a new life in Africa! Africa! The Cape.

Everything in moderation especially the diet and exercise. Blood needs food and nutrients. All of our departures from a modern world has been left behind. Perhaps we will have fruit trees. Whole orchards of them. Skies exposes all of us. The sunlight. The more we are exposed to it the more the flames of the sun burn us. It licks our skin. Sometimes in the morning, I like to walk from side to side of the boat knowing that everyone is watching me. Then I can eat my boiled egg and toast and think that the world is not so bad.

I forget what the doctor says sometimes. How many times a day must I rest, take to my bed, draw the curtains, watch what I eat? Do not eat too much protein? Do not eat much fatty and rich duck, as it will somehow end up in my blood? In a new land how will we live, how will I survive? All I know is London. All I know is London society. Now this ship. This boat sailing on the open water rocking from side to side making me feel queasy and sick to my stomach. There are good days when I can walk from one side of the ship to the next and I can believe in anything that Rufane is telling me. The children we will have. He has so much hope in him. So much love. Next to him, I am cumbersome. Next to me, he is majestic. It is as if overnight on this boat I have become very old, and frail. My bones are a frilled delicacy. I feel the cold. It is winter. It is a winter sun but my body longs for the moonlight too as much as I long for my husband Rufane smiling. I am afraid that I do not make him smile anymore.

I remember every word he said. Forget this place of weeping. It is a stranger to the heart. We will build empires of gold. She was tired of wondering if he had ever loved her at all. I am in awe of people who make a personal commitment to each other. It is becoming hazy. A new future beckons. I move silently toward it. Splendidly, avoiding the past neatly. I am dreaming. I am a child again. The cat is back on the garden wall. It is black. Sometimes it prances about, sometimes I find it sleeping, curled up in a foetal position, and sometimes it is purring when stroked between the ears. All loved up even after the ancient wisdom of eating. I pull her close to me. Unlike man, she is a friend. It is not easy to start over. All I wanted was a friend, but I hear these voices all around me. The psychiatrist stared at me in the face with a sad, defeatist's look anticipating the change in my mood and so I was cast off into the void. Sailing in the dark with every narcissistic impulse that the human condition has been afflicted with.

I am tragic. I am a tragedy in the works I am afraid. Half the time I am a scared cat. I thought that love was so noble, that it could heal anything and that the sanctity of marriage was ingenuous. They are only romanticised ideals of love. Nothing more. Nothing less. I will never leave this place. He has called it Port Elizabeth, South Africa. A part of me does not want to go but wants the order and routine of our old life. Elizabeth and Rufane Donkin invited to so and so's soiree. I am a sleeping beauty and other stories. Ghost stories. You are so brave. A voice tells me. Whispers. Sings melodically or in the dead of night out of tune. I know that much is true. Damages. Traffic. Keats is pure and part rebel. I am imagining life after twenty something and then I cannot imagine it. Feeling much more alive than I am already. There is the darkness and the light. One is more forgiving than the other is. People are moving in the dark. Stick figures behind trees. The air is wet.

Is it from my tears or from the spray of the water? While I was sleeping people were born into this universe. Souls. Souls! They did not have character traits yet. They did not live in a cynical, jaded, insensitive, intellectually driven world yet. Their personal space not invaded yet. They were not creating havoc yet. Rufane is in a state when I am in an emotional state. Hysterics and tears. He leaves the room. We have our meals separately. He tries to understand, tries to placate me. He clings too much. He loves too much. Will this new land have wild bananas and exotic fruit? Of course, we will still have our tea, which is understood. It is a kind of red bush tea and is a very good remedy for all kind of aches and pains. So, for my own sanity we have travelled a long way and come to a place where I will not have to have any kind of life here. I will just rest and rest and rest. Heaven! Paradise! Those doctors have said it would be good for me. A different lifestyle. My habits would change. We would eat as close to nature as possible.

Now I am the girl in love with the volcano. I no longer require myself as being part of the watershed system. I perform a brutal demonstration of an invisible people. Here humanity has no colour or a demonstration of an invisible people, which will leave you weak at the knees. I have made mistakes. I am not a perfect picture. You cannot always put a name to a face. I no longer keep it all locked away inside it. Some days the illness feel like a paperweight, other days I cannot see it like a shadow boxer caught between the bloodlines of the other player. A lesson in humility is learning never to let go. Is this a confession? Take me away from all of this, from all of here. I cannot live without you, but she was afraid, deathly afraid of was that the illness would still be here in the morning. That the illness would want to possess her or own her. You don't own me. Don't forget that. Soon the illness would slip away into the shadows before the sun came up and that suited her. Female writers were never prosaic about love up to a point. Even in their prose.

If she were a beautiful woman she would be vain instead she is as plain as paper. About love, even in the prose, that art, they are tools of seduction, figures of women and men who are considered glorified contemporary masters of disguise. I need my poets as I need my potatoes. The way women would need their calcium supplement and self-defence classes in the twentieth century onwards. Yes, I am a ghost now and what of it. What if I haunt and go around in my old-fashioned clothes changing the temperature in the air. I do not have to anchor myself to anything. Gravity means nothing to me and neither does your personal space. Instead, it becomes something that I become attached to. There are no footsteps when I am around. The flux or void in my eyes no longer have windows to my soul fortunately in my case. I am Elizabeth Donkin. Rufane Donkin's longsuffering wife. The acting-governor of the Cape's wife. This pageant of emotion that is coursing through my veins. What is it? This empowering feeling.

Watch how I lift the veil over the landscape of England behind me with her lush green hills. Where will I begin? With the ripples on the water, the tide, the moon and her light. What kind of light is this that reveals savages and natives to me, to us with their personal velocity? A husband and wife with their English mannerisms. There is a swelling of poetry inside my head. English poets. I am Elizabeth. There is a disharmony in the heat. I remain intrigued by them. The natives. They must think I am a pale goddess. It is a new day. It is a new land. If I lived to a ripe old age in another century then perhaps my name would have been Bessie, after Bessie Head, after South Africa had become a democracy and a much more integrated society. What would she do with him then, a husband? He would expect her to cook and clean for her. Hah! This Bessie would think to herself. Not this feminist but feminist is not even a word yet. We are in a century behind the times. It is the 1820's.

If my name was Emily and I was in a treatment centre for eating disorders perhaps this time of the evening I would be, lighting a cigarette and taking a long drag on it. Biting a nail absentmindedly. Willing myself not to cry for unfulfilled desires, children, happiness, the final test. Instead, I am a ghost with an English accent, an English ghost story. My airs and graces smelling like a rose garden. I dreamed that Rufane was perfect. He was in his own way. I was in mine. I am burdened in some ways. More than the general population. Tonight, I am on that boat again. Eating in my quarters. Alone. In rhythmic despair. Dreaming of oceanic patterns on walls.

Mmap New African Poets Series

If you have enjoyed **Of Smoke Flesh and Bone** consider these other fine books in *New African Poets Series* from **Mwanaka Media and Publishing:**

I Threw a Star in a Wine Glass by Fethi Sassi
Best New African Poets 2017 Anthology by Tendai R Mwanaka and Daniel Da Purificacao
Logbook Written by a Drifter by Tendai Rinos Mwanaka
Mad Bob Republic: Bloodlines, Bile and a Crying Child by Tendai Rinos Mwanaka
Zimbolicious Poetry Anthology Vol 1 by Tendai R Mwanaka and Edward Dzonze
Zimbolicious Anthology Vol 3: An Anthology of Zimbabwean Literature and Arts by Tendai Mwanaka
Under The Steel Yoke by Jabulani Mzinyathi
Fly in a Beehive by Thato Tshukudu
Bounding for Light by Richard Mbuthia
Sentiments by Jackson Matimba
Best New African Poets 2018 Anthology by Tendai R Mwanaka and Nsah Mala
Words That Matter by Gerry Sikazwe
The Ungendered by Delia Watterson
Ghetto Symphony by Mandla Mavolwane
Sky for a Foreign Bird by Fethi Sassi
A Portrait of Defiance by Tendai Rinos Mwanaka
When Escape Becomes the only Lover by Tendai R Mwanaka
وَيَسهَرُ اللَّيلُ عَلَى شَفَتِي...وَالغَمَام by Fethi Sassi
A Letter to the President by Mbizo Chirasha
Righteous Indignation by Jabulani Mzinyathi:
Blooming Cactus by Mikateko Mbambo
The Rhythm of Life by Olivia Ngozi Osouha

Travellers Gather Dust and Lust by Gabriel Awuah Mainoo
Chitungwiza Mushamukuru: An Anthology from Zimbabwe's Biggest Ghetto Town by Tendai Rinos Mwanaka
Because Sadness is Beautiful? by Tanaka Chidora
Poems of Resistance by John Eppel
Shades of Black by Edward Dzonze
Thoughts Hunt The Loves/Pfungwa Dzinovhima Vadiwa by Jeton Kelmendi, translation by Tendai Mwanaka
Best New African Poets 2019 Anthology by Tendai R. Mwanaka and Nsah Mala
Zimbolicious Anthology Vol 4: An Anthology of Zimbabwean Literature and Arts by Tendai Rinos Mwanaka and Jabulani Mzinyathi

Soon to be released

Writing Robotics, Africa Vs Asia Vol 2 by Tendai R Mwanaka
Zimbolicious Anthology Vol 5: An Anthology of Zimbabwean Literature and Arts by Tendai R. Mwanaka and Tembi Charles
Denga reshiri yokunze kwenyika by Fethi Sassi

https://facebook.com/MwanakaMediaAndPublishing/

www.ingramcontent.com/pod-product-compliance
Lightning Source LLC
Chambersburg PA
CBHW011952150426
43196CB00019B/2918